AINO FOLK-TALES

BY
BASIL HALL CHAMBERLAIN.

WITH INTRODUCTION
BY
EDWARD B. TYLOR, D.C.L., F.R.S.

Privately Printed

FOR
THE FOLK-LORE SOCIETY.

1888.
XXII.

List of Officers of the Society

1887-1888.

PRESIDENT.

THE RIGHT HON. THE EARL OF STRAFFORD.

VICE-PRESIDENTS.

ANDREW LANG, M.A.

W. R. S. RALSTON, M.A.

EDWARD B. TYLOR, LL.D., F.R.S.

DIRECTOR.

G. L. GOMME, F.S.A., 1, Beverley Villas, Barnes Common, S.W.

COUNCIL.

A. MACHADO Y ALVAREZ.

THE EARL BEAUCHAMP, F.S.A.

EDWARD BRABROOK, F.S.A.

DR. D. G. BRINTON

JAMES BRITTEN, F.L.S.

LOYS BRUEYRE.

MISS C. S. BURNE.

EDWARD CLODD.

PROFESSOR D. COMPARETTI.

G. L. GOMME, F.S.A.

A. GRANGER HUTT, F.S.A.

SIR JOHN LUBBOCK, Bt., F.R.S.

SIR HENRY MAINE, K.C.S.I.

REV. DR. RICHARD MORRIS.

ALFRED NUTT.

EDWARD PEACOCK, F.S.A.

Z. D. PEDROSO.

PROFESSOR A. H. SAYCE, M.A.

CAPTAIN R. C. TEMPLE.

HENRY B. WHEATLEY, F.S.A.

AUDITORS.

G. L. APPERSON.

JOHN TOLHURST, F.S.A.

LOCAL SECRETARIES.

IRELAND: G. H. KINAHAN, R.I.A.

SOUTH SCOTLAND: WILLIAM GEORGE BLACK.

NORTH SCOTLAND: REV. WALTER GREGOR.

INDIA: CAPTAIN R. C. TEMPLE.

CHINA: J. STEWART LOCKHART.

HONORARY SECRETARIES.

A. GRANGER HUTT, F.S.A., 8, Oxford Road, Kilburn, N.W.

J. J. FOSTER, 36, Alma Square, St. John's Wood, N.W.

I. – TALES ACCOUNTING FOR THE ORIGIN OF PHENOMENA.

II. – MORAL TALES.

III. — TALES OF THE PANAUMBE AND PENAUMBE CYCLE.

IV. — MISCELLANEOUS TALES.

V. — SCRAPS OF FOLK-LORE.

INTRODUCTION.

Twelve hundred years ago a Chinese historian stated that "on the eastern frontier of the land of Japan there is a barrier of great mountains, beyond which is the land of the Hairy Men." These were the Aino, so named from the word in their own language signifying "man." Over most of the country of these rude and helpless indigenes the Japanese have long since spread, only a dwindling remnant of them still inhabiting the island of Yezo. Since the early days when a couple of them were sent as curiosities to the Emperor of China their uncouth looks and habits have made them objects of interest to more civilised nations. Many European writers have described them, but hardly any with such opportunities as Mr. Basil Hall Chamberlain, Professor of Philology at the Tōkyō University, who has taken down from the Ainos the present collection of their tales, and prefaced it with an account of their ways and state of mind. It would hardly be for me to offer information on a subject so excellently handled, but the request of the Editor of the Folk-Lore Journal that I would write an Introduction enables me to draw attention to the views put forward by Professor Chamberlain in another publication,* which, being printed in Japan, may be overlooked by many English folk-lore students, even of those interested in the curious Aino problem.

* *The Language, Mythology, and Geographical Nomenclature of Japan, viewed in the light of Aino Studies.* By Basil Hall Chamberlain. Including an *Ainu Grammar* by John Batchelor. (Memoirs of the Literature College, Imperial University of Japan, No. 1.) Tōkyō: 1887.

As is well known, the hairiness of the Ainos marks them sharply off from the smooth-faced Japanese. No one can look at photographs of Ainos without admitting that the often-repeated comparison of them to bearded Russian peasants is much to the purpose. The likeness is much strengthened by the bold quasi-European features of the Ainos contrasting extremely with the Japanese type of face. Of (6.) course all this has suggested a theory of the Ainos belonging to the Aryan race; and, although the idea comes to nothing when examined strictly, its existence is an acknowledgment of the special Aino race-type. Mention must also be made of an anatomical peculiarity of the Aino skeleton, consisting of a remarkable flattening of the arm-and leg-bones. On the whole it is evident that the Ainos are an ancient race in this part of Asia, and so far isolated that anthropology has not yet the means of settling their physical connection with other Asiatic tribes. Professor Chamberlain's careful examination of the Aino language leads him to a similar result. It is made not only from his own knowledge, but with the advantage of working with the Rev. John Batchelor, who has lived as a missionary among the Ainos for years, and written the Grammar printed as a part of these Aino Studies. In structure the resemblances which the Aino presents to Japanese are outweighed by the differences; and, though it may ultimately prove to fall into a north-east Asiatic group of languages, this is so far from being made out that it is safest for the present to treat both race and language as isolated. Inasmuch as the little civilisation now possessed by the Ainos has in great measure been learnt from the Japanese, it is natural that their modern language should have picked up numbers of Japanese words, from the name of kamui which they give to their gods, down to the rice-beer or sake in which they seek continual drunkenness, now their main source of enjoyment. One purpose which their language serves is to prove how widely they once spread over the country now Japan, where place-names alone remain to indicate a former Aino population. Some of these are unmistakeably Aino, as Yamashiro, which must have meant "land of chestnut trees," and Shikyu, "place of rushes." Others, if interpreted as Japanese, have a far-fetched sense, as, for instance, the villages of Mennai and Tonami, which, if treated as Japanese, would signify "inside permission" and "hares in a row"; whereas, if taken to be originally Aino they may bear the reasonable sense of "bad stream" and "stream from the lake." The inference from records and local names, worked out with great care by Professor Chamberlain, is "that the Ainos were truly the predecessors of the Japanese all over the Archipelago. The dawn of history shows them to us living far to the south and west of their present haunts; and ever since then, century by century, we see them retreating eastwards and northwards, as steadily as the American Indian has retreated westwards under the pressure of the colonists from Europe."

As with their language, so with their folk-lore, which largely shows itself adopted from the Japanese. In the present collection the stories of the Salmon-king (34.), the Island of Women (33.), and others, are based on episodes of Japanese tales, sometimes belonging to world-wide cycles of myth, as in the theme of the mortal who eats the deadly food of Hades (35.), which has its typical example in the story of Persephone. On reading the short but curious tale *How it was settled who should rule the World* (16.), one sees at once that the cunning Fox-god has come in from the well-known fox mythology of Japan; and as to the very clever mythic episode of looking for the sunrise in the west, I find, on inquiry of a Japanese gentleman living in Oxford, Mr. Tsneta Mori, that this belongs to the tale of the Wager of the Phœnix, known to all Japanese children, and in which the Phœnix is plainly derived from China. On the other hand, there is much genuine Aino matter in the present collection. For instance, we learn from Professor Chamberlain's above-mentioned treatise why it is that Panaumbe ("on the lower course of the river") does the clever things, while Penaumbe ("on the upper course of the river") is the stupid imitator who comes to grief. It is simply the expression of the dislike and contempt of the coast Ainos, who tell the stories, for the hill Ainos further up the rivers. It is needless to mention here the many touches of Aino ideas, morals, and customs, which their stories disclose, for it is in noticing these that much of the interest consists which the reader will feel in perusing them. Their most important characteristic indeed is insisted on by Professor Chamberlain, in remarks of which the value must not be overlooked. Of all the difficulties felt by the student of folk-lore the greatest is that of judging how far those who tell and listen really believe their childish wonder-tales of talking beasts and the like, or how far they make and take them as conscious fun. We ourselves are at the latter sceptical end, and many peoples we can examine are in a halfway state, not altogether disbelieving that big stones may (8.) once have been giants, or that it is a proper incident in a hero's career to be swallowed by a monster and get out again, but at the same time admitting that after all these may be only old wives' tales. Even savage tribes under contact with civilised men are mostly in this intermediate state, and thus Professor Chamberlain's statement as to the place of folk-lore in the Aino mind, made, as it has been, under his personal scrutiny, is a document of real consequence. He satisfied himself that his Ainos were not making believe, like Europeans with nursery tales, but that the explanatory myths of natural phenomena are to them theorems of physical science, and the wonder-tales are told under the impression that they really happened. Those who maintain the serious value of folk-lore, as embodying early but quite real stages of philosophy among mankind, will be grateful for this collection, in spite of its repulsive features, as furnishing the clearest evidence that the basis of their argument is not only theoretical but actual.

Edward B. Tylor.

AINO FOLK-LORE.

By Basil Hall Chamberlain.

Prefatory Remarks.

I VISITED the island of Yezo for the third time in the summer of 1886, in order to study the Aino language, with a view to elucidate by its means the obscure problem of the geographical nomenclature of Japan. But, as is apt to happen on such occasions, the chief object of my visit soon ceased to be the only object. He who would learn a language must try to lisp in it, and more especially must he try to induce the natives to chatter in it in his presence. Now in Yezo, subjects of discourse are few. The Ainos stand too low in the scale of humanity to have any notion of the civilised art of "making conversation." When, therefore, the fishing and the weather are exhausted, the European sojourner in one of their dreary, filthy seaside hamlets will find himself,—at least I found myself,—sadly at a loss for any further means of setting his native companions' tongues in motion. It is then that fairy-tales come to the rescue. The Ainos would not suggest the idea themselves. To suggest ideas is not their habit. But they are delighted to follow it when suggested.

Simply to repeat something which they have known by heart ever since the days of their childhood is not such an effort to their easily-tired brains as is the keeping up of a conversation with one who speaks their language imperfectly. Their tongues are at once loosened.

In my own case, I found myself, after a short time, listening to the stories for their own sake,—not merely as linguistic exercises; and I ventured to include a few of them in the "Memoir on the Ainos" which was published a few months ago by the Imperial University of Japan. Some remarks in a review of this "Memoir," contained in Nature of the 12th May, 1887, have encouraged me to believe that anthropologists and comparative mythologists may be interested in having laid before them something more than mere samples of the mental products of a people which is interesting for three reasons,— interesting because its domain once extended over the entire Japanese archipelago, interesting because absolutely nothing certain is known as to its origin and affinities, interesting because it is, so to speak, almost at its last gasp. I have, therefore, now collected and classified all the tales that were communicated to me by Ainos, in Aino, during my last stay in the island, and more latterly in Tōkyō, when, by the kind assistance of the President of the University, Mr. H. Watanabe, an exceptionally intelligent Aino was procured from the North, and spent a month in my house. These tales form the paper which I now have the honour to offer for the acceptance of your learned Society.

It would, no doubt, be possible to treat the subject of Aino folk-lore in great detail. The gloss might easily be made longer than the text. Each story might be analysed according to the method proposed by the Folk-Lore Society; a "survey of incidents" might be appended to each, as in Messrs. Steel and Temple's charming "Wide-Awake Stories," from the Punjab and Cashmere. More interesting to the anthropologist than such mechanical dissection of each tale considered as an independent entity would be the attempt to unravel the affinities of these Aino tales. How many of them, what parts of them, are original? How many of them are borrowed, and whence?

To carry out such an investigation with that completeness which would alone give it serious value, would necessitate a greater expenditure of time than my duties will allow of, perhaps also a fund of multifarious knowledge which I do not possess. I would, therefore, merely suggest in passing that the probabilities of the case are in favour of the Ainos having borrowed from their only clever neighbours, the Japanese. (The advent of the Russians is so recent that they need hardly be counted in this connection.) The reasons for attributing to the Japanese, rather than to the Ainos, the prior possession (which, by the way, by no means implies the invention) of the tales common to both races, are partly general, partly special. Thus it is a priori likely that the stupid and barbarous will be taught by the clever and educated, not the clever and educated by the stupid and barbarous. On the other hand, as I have elsewhere demonstrated, a comparative study of the languages of the two peoples shows clearly that this a priori view is fully borne out so far as far as the linguistic domain is concerned. The same remark applies to social customs. Even in religion, the most conservative of all institutions, especially among barbarians, the Ainos have suffered Japanese influence to intrude itself. It is Japanese rice-beer, under its Japanese name of sake, which they offer in libations to their gods. Their very word for "prayer" seems to be archaic Japanese. A mediæval Japanese hero, Yoshitsune, is generally allowed to be held in religious reverence by them. The idea of earthquakes being caused by the wriggling of a gigantic fish under the earth is shared by the Ainos with the Japanese and with several other races.

At the same time, the general tenour and tendency of the tales and traditions of the Ainos wear a widely different aspect from that which characterises the folk-lore of Japan. The Ainos, in their humble way, are addicted to moralising and to speculating on the origin of things. A perusal of the following tales will show that a surprisingly large number of them are attempts to explain some natural phenomenon, or to exemplify some simple precept. In fact they are science,—physical science and moral science,—at a very early stage. The explanations given in these tales completely satisfy the adult Aino mind of the present day. The Aino fairy-tales are not, as ours are, survivals from an earlier stage of thought. They spring out of the present state of thought. Even if not invented of recent years they fit in with the present Aino view of things,—so much so, that an Aino who recounts one of his stories does so under the impression that he is narrating an actual event. He does not "make believe" like the European nurse, even like the European child, who has always, in some nook or corner of his mind, a presentiment of the scepticism of his later years.

So far as I can judge, that "disease of language"

which we call metaphor, and which is held by some great authorities to have been the chief factor in the fabrication of Aryan myth, has no place in Aino fairyland; neither have the phenomena of the weather attracted more attention than other things. But I speak subject to correction. Perhaps it is not wise to invite controversy on such a point unless one is well armed for the fight.

Failing an elaborate analysis of the Aino fairy-tales, and a discussion of their origin and affinities, what I venture to offer for your Society's acceptance is the simple text of the tales themselves, rendered into English. Nine of them have already been printed in the Aino "Memoir" already referred to. One has been printed (but not quite in its genuine form, which decency was supposed to forbid) at the end of Mr. Batchelor's grammar included in the same "Memoir." All the others are now given to the world for the first time, never having yet appeared in any language, not even in Japanese.

I would draw special attention to the character of the translation, as being an absolutely literal one in the case of all those stories which I originally wrote down in Aino from the dictation of native informants. As time pressed, however, I sometimes had the story told me more rapidly, and wrote it down afterwards in English only, but never more than a few hours afterwards. In such cases, though every detail is preserved, the rendering is of course not actually literal. This, and the fact that there were several informants, will account for the difference of style between the various stories. I have appended to each story either the words "translated literally," or the words "written down from memory," together with the date and the name of the informant, in order that those who use the collection may know exactly what it is that they are handling. In all such matters, absolute accuracy, absolute literalness, wherever attainable, is surely the one thing necessary. Not all the charm of diction, not all the ingenious theories in the world, can for a moment be set in the balance against rigid exactness, even if some of the concomitants of rigid exactness are such as to spoil the subject for popular treatment. The truth, the stark naked truth, the truth without so much as a loin-cloth on, should surely be the investigator's sole aim when, having discovered a new set of facts, he undertakes to present them to the consideration of the scientific world.

Of course Aino tales, like other tales, may also be treated from a literary point of view. Some of the tales of the present collection, prettily illustrated with pictures by Japanese artists, and altered, expurgated, and arranged virginibus puerisque, are at the present moment being prepared by Messrs. Ticknor & Co., of Boston, who thought with me that such a venture might please our little ones both in England and in the United States. But such things have no scientific value. They are not meant to have any. They are mere juvenile literature, whose English dressing-up has as little relation to the barbarous original as the Paris fashions have to the anatomy of the human frame.

The present paper, on the contrary, is intended for the sole perusal of the anthropologist and ethnologist, who would be deprived of one of the best means of judging of the state of the Aino mind if the hideous indecencies of the original were omitted, or its occasional ineptitude furbished up. Aino mothers, lulling their babies to sleep, as they rock them in the cradle hung over the kitchen fire, use words, touch on subjects which we never mention; and that precisely is a noteworthy characteristic. The innocent savage is not found in Aino-land, if indeed he is to be found anywhere. The Aino's imagination is as prurient as that of any Zola, and far more outspoken. Pray, therefore, put the blame on him, if much of the language of the present collection is such as it is not usual to see in print. Aino stories and Aino conversation are the intellectual counterpart of the dirt, the lice, and the skin-diseases which cover Aino bodies.

For the four-fold classification of the stories, no importance is claimed. It was necessary to arrange them somehow; and the division into "Tales Accounting for the Origin of Phenomena," "Moral Tales," "Tales of the Panaumbe and Penaumbe Cycle," and "Miscellaneous Tales," suggested itself as a convenient working arrangement. The "Scraps of Folk-Lore," which have been added at the end, may perhaps be considered out of place in a collection of tales. But I thought it better to err on the side of inclusion than on that of exclusion. For it may be presumed that the object of any such investigation is rather to gain as minute an acquaintance as possible with the mental products of the people studied, than scrupulously to conform to any system.

There must be a large number of Aino fairy-tales besides those here given, as the chief tellers of stories, in Aino-land as in Europe, are the women, and I had mine from men only, the Aino women being much too shy of male foreigners for it to be possible to have much conversation with them. Even of the tales I myself heard, several were lost through the destruction of certain papers,—among others at least three of the Panaumbe and Penaumbe Cycle, which I do not trust myself to reconstruct from memory at this distance of time. Many precious hours were likewise wasted, and much material rendered useless, by the national vice of drunkenness. A whole month at Hakodate was spoilt in this way, and nothing obtained from an Aino named Tomtare, who had been procured for me by the kindness of H. E. the Governor of Hakodate. One can have intercourse with men who smell badly, and who suffer, as almost all Ainos do, from lice and from a variety of disgusting skin-diseases. It is a mere question of endurance and of disinfectants. But it is impossible to obtain information from a drunkard. A third reason for the comparatively small number of tales which it is possible to collect during a limited period of intercourse is the frequency of repetitions. No doubt such repetitions have a confirmatory value, especially when the repetition is of the nature of a variant. Still, one would willingly spare them for the sake of new tales.

The Aino names appended to the stories are those of the men by whom they were told to me, viz. Penri, the aged chief of Piratori; Ishanashte of Shumunkot; Kannariki of Poropet (Jap. Horobetsu); and Kuteashguru of Sapporo. Tomtare of Yūrap does not appear for the reason mentioned above, which spoilt all his usefulness. The only mythological names which appear are Okikurumi, whom the Ainos regard as having been their civilizer in very ancient times, his sister-wife Turesh, or Tureshi[hi] and his henchman Samayunguru. The "divine symbols," of which such constant mention is made in the tales, are the inao or whittled sticks frequently described in books of travels.

Basil Hall Chamberlain.

Miyanoshita, Japan,
20th July, 1887.

I. – TALES ACCOUNTING FOR THE ORIGIN OF PHENOMENA.

1. – The Rat and the Owl.*

An owl had put by for next day the remains of something dainty which he had to eat. But a rat stole it, whereupon the owl was very angry, and went off to the rat's house, and threatened to kill him. But the rat apologised, saying: "I will give you this gimlet and tell you how you can obtain from it pleasure far greater than the pleasure of eating the food which I was so rude as to eat up. Look here! you must stick the gimlet with the sharp point upwards in the ground at the foot of this tree; then go to the top of the tree yourself, and slide down the trunk."

Then the rat went away, and the owl did as the rat had instructed him. But, sliding down on to the sharp gimlet, his anus was transfixed, and he suffered great pain, and, in his grief and rage, went off to kill the rat. But again the rat met him with apologies, and, as a peace-offering, gave him a cap for his head.

These events account for the thick cap of erect feathers which the owl wears to this day, and also for the enmity between the owl and the rat.

(Written down from memory. Told by Ishanashte, 25th November, 1886.)

* The Aino name here used (*ahunrashambe*) denotes a horned species.

2. – *The Loves of the Thunder-Gods.*

Two young thunder-gods, sons of the chief thunder-god, fell violently in love with the same Aino woman. Said one of them to the other, in a joking way: "I will become a flea, so as to be able to hop into her bosom." Said the other: "I will become a louse, so as to be able to stay always in her bosom."

"Are those your wishes?" cried their father, the chief thunder-god. "You shall be taken at your word"; and forthwith the one of them who had said he would become a flea was turned into a flea, while he who said he would become a louse was turned into a louse. Hence all the fleas and lice that exist at the present day.

This accounts for the fact that, whenever there is a thunder-storm, fleas jump out of all sorts of places where there were none to be seen before.

(Written down from memory. Told by Ishanashte,
27th November, 1886.)

3. – *Why Dogs cannot speak.*

Formerly dogs could speak. Now they cannot. The reason is that a dog, belonging to a certain man a long time ago, inveigled his master into the forest under the pretext of showing him game, and there caused him to be devoured by a bear. Then the dog went home to his master's widow, and lied to her, saying: "My master has been killed by a bear. But when he was dying he commanded me to tell you to marry me in his stead." The widow knew that the dog was lying. But he kept on urging her to marry him. So at last, in her grief and rage, she threw a handful of dust into his open mouth. This made him unable to speak any more, and therefore no dogs can speak even to this very day.

(Written down from memory. Told by Ishanashte,
29th November, 1886.)

4. – *Why the Cock cannot fly.*

When the Creator had finished creating the world, and had returned to the sky, he sent down the cock to see whether the world was good or not, with orders to come back at once. But the world was so beautiful, that the cock, unable to tear himself away, kept lingering on from day to day. At last, after a long time, he was on his way flying back up to the sky. But God, angry with him for his disobedience, stretched forth his hand, and beat him down to earth, saying: "You are not wanted in the sky any more."

That is why, to this very day, the cock cannot fly high.

(Written down from memory. Told by Penri,
18th July, 1886.)

5. – *The Origin of the Hare.*

Suddenly there was a large house on the top of a mountain, wherein were six people beautifully arrayed, but constantly quarrelling. Whence they came was unknown. Thereupon Okikurumi came and said: "Oh! you bad hares! you wicked hares! who does not know your origin? The children in the sky were pelting each other with snowballs, and the snowballs fell into the world of men. As it would be a pity to waste anything that falls from the sky, the snowballs were turned into hares, and those hares are you. You, who dwell in this world, which belongs to me, should not quarrel. What is it that you are making such a noise about?"

With these words, Okikurumi seized a fire-brand, and beat each of the six with it in turn. Thereupon all the hares ran away. This is the origin of the hare[-god]; and for this reason the body of the hare is white because made of snow, while its ears — which are the place where it was charred by the fire-brand, — are black.

(Translated literally. Told by Penri,
10th July, 1886.)

6. – *The Position of the Private Parts.*

At the beginning of the world it had been the Creator's intention to place both men's and women's genitals on their foreheads so that they might be able to procreate children easily. But the otter made a mistake in conveying the message to that effect; and that is how the genitals come to be in the inconvenient place they are now in.

(Written down from memory. Told by Ishanashte,
11th July, 1886.)

7. – *The Reason for there being no Fixed Time for Human Beings to copulate.*

Anciently the Creator summoned all the birds and beasts, the gods and devils together, in order to instruct them on the subject of copulation. So the birds and all the others of every sort assembled, and learnt from the Creator when to copulate, and when to give birth to their young.

Then the Creator said to the horse: "Oh! thou divine ancestor of horses! It will be well for thee to copulate one spring, and to give birth to thy young in the spring of the following year; and thou mayest eat any of the grass that may grow in any land." At these words, the horse was delighted, and forthwith trotted out. But, as he rose, he kicked God in the forehead. So God was very angry, and pressed his hand to his head, so much did it hurt him.

Meanwhile, the ancestor of men came in, and asked saying: "How about me? When shall I copulate?" To which God, being still angry, replied: "Whenever you like!" For this reason, that race of creatures which is called man copulate at all times.

(Translated literally. Told by Ishanashte, 12th July, 1886).

8. – *The Owl and the Tortoise.*

The tortoise[-god] in the sea and the owl[-god] on land were very intimate. The tortoise spoke thus: "Your child is a boy. My child is a girl. So it will be good for us to unite them in marriage. If I send into the river the fish that there are in the sea your son and my daughter, being both of them enabled to eat fish, will possess the world." Thus spoke the tortoise. The owl was greatly obliged. For this reason, the child of the tortoise and the child of the owl became husband and wife. For this reason, the owl, without the least hesitation, eats every fish that comes into the river.

(Translated literally. Told by Penri,
15th July, 1886.)

9. – How a Man got the better of two Foxes.

A man went into the mountains to get bark to make rope with, and found a hole. To this hole there came a fox, who spoke as follows, though he was a fox, in human language: "I know of something from which great profit may be derived. Let us go to the place to-morrow!" To which the fox inside the hole replied as follows: "What profitable thing do you allude to? After hearing about it, I will go with you if it sounds likely to be profitable; and if not, not." The fox outside spoke thus: "The profitable thing to be done is this. I will come here to-morrow about the time of the mid-day meal. You must be waiting for me then, and we will go off together. If you take the shape of a horse, and we go off together, I taking the shape of a man and riding on your back, we can go down to the shore, where dwell human beings possessed of plenty of food and all sorts of other things. As there is sure to be among the people some one who wants a horse, I will sell you to him who thus wants a horse. I can then buy a quantity of precious things and of food. Then I shall run away; and you, having the appearance of a horse, will be led out to eat grass, and be tied up somewhere on the hillside. Then, if I come and help you to escape, and we divide the food and the precious things equally between us, it will be profitable for both of us." Thus spoke the fox outside the hole; and the fox inside the hole was very glad, and said: "Come and fetch me early to-morrow, and we will go off together."

The man was hidden in the shade of the tree, and had been listening. Then the fox who had been standing outside went away, and the man, too, went home for the night. But he came back next day to the mouth of the hole, and spoke thus, imitating the voice of the fox whom he had heard speaking outside the hole the day before: "Here I am. Come out at once! If you will turn into a horse, we will go down to the shore." The fox came out. It was a big fox. The man said: "I have come already turned into a man. If you turn into a horse, it will not matter even if we are seen by other people." The fox shook itself, and became a large chestnut [lit. red] horse. Then the two went off together, and came to a very rich village, plentifully provided with everything. The man said: "I will sell this horse to anybody who wants one." As the horse was a very fine one, every one wanted to buy it. So the man bartered it for a quantity of food and precious things, and then went away.

Now the horse was such a peculiarly fine one that its new owner did not like to leave it out-of-doors, but always kept it in the house. He shut the door, and he shut the window, and cut grass to feed it with. But though he fed it, it could not (being really a fox) eat grass at all. All it wanted to eat was fish. After about four days it was like to die. At last it made its escape through the window and ran home; and, arriving at the place where the other fox lived, wanted to kill it. But it discovered that the trick had been played, not by its companion fox, but by the man. So both the foxes were very angry, and consulted about going to find the man and kill him.

But though the two foxes had decided thus, the man came and made humble excuses, saying: "I came the other day, because I had overheard you two foxes plotting; and then I cheated you. For this I humbly beg your pardon. Even if you do kill me, it will do no good. So henceforward I will brew rice-beer for you, and set up the divine symbols for you, and worship you,—worship you for ever. In this way you will derive greater profit than you would derive from killing me. Fish, too, whenever I make a good catch, I will offer to you as an act of worship. This being so, the creatures called men shall worship you for ever."

The foxes, hearing this, said: "That is capital, we think. That will do very well." Thus spake the foxes. Thus does it come about that all men, both Japanese and Aino, worship the fox. So it is said.

(Translated literally. Told by Ishanashte, 15th July, 1886.)

10. – *The Man who Married the Bear-Goddess.*

There was a very populous village. It was a village having both plenty of fish and plenty of venison. It was a place lacking no kind of food. Nevertheless, once upon a time, a famine set in. There was no food, no venison, no fish, nothing to eat at all; there was a famine. So in that populous village all the people died.

Now the village chief was a man who had two

children, a boy and a girl. After a time, only those two children remained alive. Now the girl was the older of the two, and the boy was the younger. The girl spoke thus: "As for me, it does not matter even if I do die, since I am a girl. But you, being a boy, can, if you like, take up our father's inheritance. So you should take these things with you, use them to buy food with, eat it, and live." So spoke the girl, and took out a bag made of cloth, and gave it to him.

Then the boy went out on to the sand, and walked along the sea-shore. When he had walked on the sand for a long time, he saw a pretty little house a short way inland. Near it was lying the carcase of a large whale. The boy went to the house, and after a time entered it. On looking around, he saw a man of divine appearance. The man's wife, too, looked like a goddess, and was dressed altogether in black raiment. The man was dressed altogether in speckled raiment. The boy went in, and stood by the door. The man said to him: "Welcome to you, whencesoever you may have come." Afterwards a lot of the whale's flesh was boiled, and the boy was feasted on it. But the woman never looked towards him. Then the boy went out and fetched his parcel, which he had left outside. He brought in the bag made of cloth which had been given to him by his sister, and opened its mouth. On taking out and looking at the things inside it, they were found to be very precious treasures. "I will give you these treasures in payment for the food," said the boy, and gave them to that divine-looking man-of-the-house. The god, having looked at them, said: "They are very beautiful treasures." He said again: "You need not have paid me for the food. But I will take these treasures of yours, carry them to my [other] house, and bring you my own treasures in exchange for them. As for this whale's flesh, you can eat as much of it as you like, without payment." Having said this, he went off with the lad's treasures.

Then the lad and the woman remained together. After a time the woman turned to the lad, and said: "You lad! listen to me when I speak. I am the bear-goddess. This husband of mine is the dragon-god. There is no one so jealous as he is. Therefore did I not look towards you, because I knew that he would be jealous if I looked towards you. Those treasures of yours are treasures which even the gods do not possess. It is because he is delighted to get them that he has taken them with him to counterfeit them and bring you mock treasures. So when he shall have brought those treasures and shall display them, you must speak thus: 'We need not exchange treasures. I wish to buy the woman!' If you speak thus, he will go angrily away, because he is such a jealous man. Then afterwards we can marry each other, which will be very pleasant. That is how you must speak." That was what the woman said.

Then, after a certain time, the man of divine appearance came back grinning. He came bringing two sets of treasures, the treasures which were treasures and his own other treasures. The god spoke thus: "You, lad! As I have brought the treasures which are your treasures, it will be well to exchange them for my treasures." The boy spoke thus: "Though I should like to have treasures also, I want your wife even more than I want the treasures; so please give me your wife instead of the treasures." Thus spoke the lad.

He had no sooner uttered the words than he was

stunned by a clap of thunder above the house. On looking around him, the house was gone, and only he and the goddess were left together. He came to his senses. The treasures were there also. Then the woman spoke thus: "What has happened is that my dragon-husband has gone away in a rage, and has therefore made this noise, because you and I wish to be together. Now we can live together." Thus spoke the goddess. Afterwards they lived together. This is why the bear is a creature half like a human being.

(Translated literally. Told by Ishanashte,
9th November, 1886.)

11. – *The two Foxes, the Mole, and the Crows.*

Two brother foxes consulted together thus: "It would be fun for us to go down among men, and assume human shape." So they made treasures and they made garments out of the leaves of various trees, and they made various things to eat and cakes out of the gum which comes out of trees. But the mole[-god] saw them making all these preparations. So the mole made a place like a human village, and placed himself in it under the disguise of a very old man. The foxes came to that village; they came to the very old man's house. And the mole himself made beautiful treasures and made garments out of various herbs and leaves of trees; and, taking mulberries and grapes from the tops of the trees, he made good food. On the arrival of the foxes, the mole invited all the crows in the place and all sorts of birds. He gave them human shape, and placed them as owners in the houses of the village. Then the mole, as chief of the village, was a very old man.

Then the foxes came, having assumed the shape of men. They thought the place was a human village. The old chief bought all the things which the foxes had brought on their backs, all their treasures and all their food. Then the old man displayed to them his own beautiful treasures. The old man displayed all his beautiful things, his garments. The foxes were much pleased. Then the old man spoke thus: "Oh you strangers! as there is a dance in my village, it will be well for you to see it." Then all the people in the village danced all sorts of dances. But at last, owing to their being birds, they began to fly upwards, notwithstanding their human shape. The foxes saw this, and were much amused. The foxes ate both of the mulberries and of the grapes. They tasted very good. It was great fun, too, to see the dancing. Afterwards they went home.

The foxes, thought thus: "What is nicer even than treasures is the delicious food which human beings have. As we do not know what it is, let us go again and buy some more of it." So they again made treasures out of herbs. Then they again went down to that village. The mole was in a golden house—a large house. He was alone in it, having sent all the crows and the rest away. As the foxes entered the house and looked about them, they saw a very venerable god. The god spoke thus: "Oh! you foxes; because you had assumed human shape, you made all sorts of counterfeit treasures. I saw all that you did. It is by me, and because of this, that you are brought here. You think this is a human village; but it is the village of me, your master the mole. It seems you constantly do all sorts of bad things. If you do so, it is very wrong; so do not assume human shape any more. If you will cease to assume human shape, you may henceforth eat your fill of these mulberries and grapes. You and your companions the crows may eat together of the mulberries and of all fruits at the top of the trees, which the crows cause to drop down. This will be much more profitable for you than to assume human shape." Thus spoke the mole.

Owing to this, the foxes left off assuming human shape, and, from that time forward, ate as they pleased of the mulberries and the grapes. When the crows let any drop, they went underneath the trees and ate them. They became very friendly together.

(Translated literally. Told by Ishanashte,
11th November, 1886.)

12. – The Stolen Charm.

A very rich man kept a puppy and a fox-cub. Besides these he possessed a tiny silver model of a ship,—a charm given to him by some god, what god I know not. One day this charm was stolen, and could nowhere be found. The rich man was so violently grieved at this, that he lay down and refused all food, and was like to die. Meanwhile the puppy and the fox-cub played about in his room. But when they saw, after some time, that the man was really going to die, the fox-cub said to the puppy: "If our master dies, we shall die of hunger too; so we had better search for the charm." So they consulted as to the best way to search for it; and at last the fox-cub was struck by the idea that the ogre who lived at the top of the large mountain that stands at the end of the world might have stolen the charm and put it into his box. The fox-cub seemed to see that this had really happened. So the two little animals determined to go and rescue the charm from the ogre. But they knew that they could not accomplish this alone, and resolved to add the rat[-god] to their number. So they invited the rat, and the three went off, dancing merrily.

Now the ogre was always looking steadily in the direction of the sick rich man, hoping that he would die. So he did not notice the approach of the fox-cub, the dog, and the rat. So when they reached the ogre's house, the rat, with the help of the fox-cub, scooped out a passage under and into the house, by which all three made their way in. They then decided that it must be left to the rat to get hold of the charm by nibbling a hole in the box in which it was kept. Meanwhile the fox-cub assumed the shape of a little boy, and the puppy that of a little girl, — two beautiful little creatures who danced and went through all sorts of antics, much to the amusement of the ogre. The ogre was, however, suspicious as to how they had come into the house, and whence they had come, for the doors were not open. So he determined just to divert himself awhile by watching their frolics, and then to kill them. Meanwhile the rat had nibbled a hole in the box. Then getting into it, he rescued the charm, and went out again through the passage in the ground. The little boy and girl disappeared too; how, the ogre could not tell. He made to pursue them through the door, when he saw them fleeing. But on second thoughts he came to the conclusion that, having once been taken in by a fox, there was no use in further endeavours. So he did not follow the three animals as they fled away.

They returned to the village; the puppy and the fox-cub to their master's house, the rat to its own place. The puppy and the fox-cub took home with them the charm, and placed it by their master's pillow, playing about near him, and pulling his clothes a little with their teeth. At length he lifted his head and saw the charm. Then he worshipped it with great joy and gratitude. Afterwards the fox-cub and the puppy caused him to see in a dream how the charm had been recovered through the rat's assistance. So he worshipped the rat also.

For this reason the Ainos do not think so very badly of the rat after all. The fox, too, though often pursued by dogs, will sometimes make friends with them; and even when a dog is pursuing a fox, it will not bite the latter if it turns its face towards the pursuer.

(Written down from memory. Told by Ishanashte, 21st November, 1886.)

13. – The Fox, the Otter, and the Monkey.

In very ancient days, at the beginning of the world, there were a fox, an otter, and a monkey, all three of whom lived on the most intimate terms of friendship.

One day the fox spoke to the other two as follows: "What do you say to our going off somewhere, and stealing food and treasures from the Japanese?" His two companions having consented, they all went together to a distant place, and stole a bag of beans, a bag of salt, and a mat from the house of a very rich man. When they had come home with their plunder, the fox said: "Otter! you had better take the salt, for it will be useful to you in salting the fish which you catch in the water when you go fishing. Monkey! do you take the mat; it will be very useful for you to make your children dance upon. As for myself, I will take the bag of beans."

After this, all three retired to their respective houses; and a little later the otter went to the river to fish. But, as he took his bag of salt with him when he made the plunge, all the salt was melted in a moment, to his great disappointment. The monkey was equally unlucky; for, having taken his mat and spread it on the top of a tree, and made his children dance there, the children fell, and were dashed to pieces on the ground below.

The monkey and the otter, enraged by the misfortunes which the fox's wiles had brought upon them, now joined together in order to fight the fox. So the latter took a lot of beans out of his bag, chewed them to a pulp, smeared all his body with the paste, and lay down pretending to be very ill. And when the otter and the monkey came and made to kill him, he said: "See to what a pitiful plight I am reduced! As a punishment for having deceived you, my whole body is now covered with boils, and I am on the point of death. There is no need for you to kill me. Go away! I am dying fast enough." The monkey looked, and saw that the fox seemed to be speaking the truth. So he went testily away, across the sea to Japan. That is the reason why there are no monkeys in the land of the Ainos.

(Written down from memory. Told by Ishanashte, 11th July, 1886.)

14. – The Fox and the Tiger. – (No. I.)

Said the tiger to the fox: "Let us run a race from the top of the world to the bottom of the world, and he who wins it shall be lord of the world!" The fox agreed, and off the tiger bounded, but without noticing that the fox had caught hold of his tail so as to get pulled along by him. Just as the tiger was about to reach the other end, he suddenly whisked round, in order to jeer at the fox, whom he believed to be far behind. But this motion exactly threw the fox safely on to the far end, so that he was able to call out to the astonished tiger: "Here I am. What are you so long about?"

For this reason there are no tigers in Aino-land.

(No. II.)

Said the tiger to the fox: "You are said to be the craftiest of all creatures. Let us now enter into rivalry, and see which of us can roar the loudest; for to him shall belong the chieftainship of the world." The fox consented, and the two stood up alongside of each other. But as it was for the tiger to roar first, he remained standing up, and did not notice how the fox scraped a hole with his paws to hide his head in, so that his ears might not be stunned by the tiger's roaring.

Well, the tiger roared a roar which he thought must be heard from the top of the world to the bottom of the world, and must certainly stun the fox. But the fox, as soon as he knew the tiger's roar to be at an end, jumped up out of the hole where he had been hiding his ears, and said: "Why! I hardly heard you. You can surely roar louder than that. You had better try again."

The tiger was very angry at this; for he had expected that the fox would be stunned to death. However he resolved to make another still more tremendous effort. He did so, while the fox again hid his head in the hole; and the tiger burst his inside in the attempt.

For this reason there are no tigers in Aino-land. For this reason, also, foxes are crafty and eloquent even at the present day.

(Written down from memory. Told by Ishanashte,
27th November, 1886.)

15. – *The Punishment of Curiosity.*

In very ancient days, when the world had just been made, everything was still unsettled and dangerous. The crust of the earth was thin, and all was burning beneath. For this reason the people did not dare to venture outside of their huts even to obtain food: for they would have scorched their feet. So they were fed by the god Okikurumi, who used to fish for them, and then send round his wife Turesh with what he had caught. But he commanded the people to ask no questions, and never to attempt to look at Turesh's face. But one day an Aino in one of the huts was not content with being fed for nothing, and disobeyed Okikurumi's commands. He wished to see who the woman was that came round every day with food. So he waited till her hand was stretched in at the window, seized hold of it, and pulled her in by main force. She screamed and struggled; and, when she was inside the hut, she turned into a wriggling, writhing dragon. The sky darkened, the thunder crashed, the dragon vanished, and the hut was consumed by lightning. Okikurumi was very angry at what the man had done. So he left off feeding the people, and went away, none, knew whither. That is why the Ainos have been poor and miserable ever since that time.

(Written down from memory. Told by Kuteashguru,
July, 1886.)

16. – *How it was settled who should rule the World.*

When the Creator had finished creating this world of men, the good and the bad gods were all mixed together promiscuously, and began disputing for the possession of the world. They disputed, — the bad gods wanting to be at the head of the government of this world, and the good gods likewise wanting to be at the head. So the following arrangement was agreed to: Whoever, at the time of sunrise, should be the first to see the luminary, should rule the world. If the bad gods should be the first to see it rise, then they should rule; and if the good gods should be the first, then they should rule. Thereupon both the bad Gods and the brilliant gods looked towards the place where the luminary was to rise. But the fox[-god] alone stood looking towards the west. After a little time, the fox cried out: "I see the sunrise." On the gods, both bad and good, turning round and gazing, they saw in truth the refulgence of the luminary in the west. This is the cause for which the brilliant gods rule the world.

(Translated literally. Told by Ishanashte, 10th July, 1886.)

17. – The Man who lost his Wife.

A man had lost his wife, and was searching for her everywhere, over hill and dale, forest and sea-shore. At last he came to a wide plain, on which stood an oak-tree. Going up to it he found it to be not so much an oak-tree as a house, in which dwelt a kind-looking old man. Said the old man: "I am the god of the oak-tree. I know of your loss, and have seen your faithful search. Rest here awhile, and refresh yourself by eating and smoking. After that, if you hope to find your wife again, you must obey my orders, which are as follows: Take this golden horse, get on his back, fly up on him to the sky, and, when you get there, ride about the streets, constantly singing."

So the man mounted the horse, which was of pure gold. The saddle and all the trappings were of gold also. As soon as he was in the saddle, the horse flew up to the sky. There the man found a world like ours, but more beautiful. There was an immense city in it; and up and down the streets of that city, day after day, he rode, singing all the while. Every one in the sky stared at him, and all the people put their hands to their noses, saying: "How that creature from the lower world stinks!" At last the stench became so intolerable to them that the chief god of the sky came and told him that he should be made to find his wife if only he would go away. Thereupon the man flew back to earth on his golden horse. Alighting at the foot of the oak-tree, he said to the oak-god: "Here am I. I did as you bade me. But I did not find my wife." "Wait a moment," said the oak-god; "you do not know what a tumult has been caused by your visit to the sky, neither have I yet told you that it was a demon who stole your wife. This demon, looking up from hell below, was so much astonished to see and hear you riding up and down the streets of heaven singing, that his gaze is still fixed in that direction. I will profit hereby to go round quietly, while his attention is absorbed, and let your wife out of the box in which he keeps her shut up."

The oak-god did as he had promised. He brought back the woman, and handed over both her and the gold horse to the man, saying: "Do not use this horse to make any more journeys to the sky. Stay on earth, and breed from it." The couple obeyed his commands, and became very rich. The gold horse gave birth to two horses, and these two bred likewise, till at last horses filled all the land of the Ainos.

(Written down from memory. Told by Ishanashte, 21st July, 1886.)

18. — *The First Appearance of the Horse in Aino-land.*

A very beautiful woman had a husband. He was a very skilful fellow. Once he went to the mountains, and disappeared. But at night he returned, bearing a deer on his back. After feasting on the deer, they went to bed. But in the middle of the night, the woman wept and screamed, saying: "This man is not my husband. Though with shame, I will declare the fact as it is. His penis is so big, so big, so big, that it will not get into my vagina; and if it did get in, I should die."

Alarmed by her cries, the neighbours ran out, and came into her house; and one strong fellow took a stick, and beat the husband, saying: "You must be some sort of devil," whereupon the husband turned into a horse, and ran away neighing. Afterwards he was beaten to death.

The truth was that the husband had been killed and supplanted by the horse. That was the first the Ainos saw of horses. In ancient days every sort of creature could thus assume human shape. So it is said.

(Translated literally. Told by Penri, 12th July, 1886.)

19. – Sunrise.

When the sun rises at the head of the world [i.e. in the east], a devil tries to swallow it. But some one thrusts two or three crows or foxes into the devil's mouth. Meanwhile the sun mounts on high. The creatures, than which there are none more numerous in this world, are the crows and the foxes. That is why things are thus. In return for this service of theirs, the crows and foxes share in all man's eatables. It is because of the above fact.

(Translated literally. Told by Penri, 13th July, 1886.)

20. – *The Sex of the Two Luminaries.*

Formerly it was the female luminary that came out at night. But she was so greatly shocked at the immoralities which she saw going on out of doors among the grass, that she exchanged with the male luminary, who, being a man, did not care so much. So now the sun is a female deity, and the moon is a male deity. But surely the sun must be often shocked at what she sees going on even in the day-time, when the young people are in the open among the grass.

(Written down from memory. Told *by Ishanashte,
November, 1886.)*

II. – MORAL TALES.

21. – The Kind Giver and the Grudging Giver.

A certain man had laid his net across the river; having laid his net, he killed a quantity of fish. Meanwhile there came a raven, and perched beside him. It seemed to be greatly hungering after the fish. It was much to be pitied. So the fisherman washed one of the fish, and threw it to the raven. The raven ate the fish with great joy. Afterwards the raven came again. Though it was a raven, it spoke thus, just like a human being: "I am very grateful for having been fed on fish by you. If you will come with me to my old father, he too will thank you. So you had better come."

The man went with the raven. Being a raven, it flew through the air. The man followed it on foot. After they had gone a long way, they came to a large house. When they got there, the raven went into the house. The man went in also. When he looked, it appeared like a human being in form, though it was a raven. There were also a divine old man and a divine old woman besides the divine girl. This girl was she who had led the man hither. The divine old man spoke thus: "I am very grateful to you. As I am very grateful to you for feeding my daughter with good fish, I have had you brought here in order to reward you." Thus spoke the divine old man.

Then there were a gold puppy and a silver puppy. Both these puppies were given to the man. The divine old man spoke thus: "Though I should give you treasures, it would be useless. But if I give you these puppies, you will be greatly benefited. As for the excrements of these two puppies, the gold puppy excretes gold and the silver puppy excretes silver. This being so, you will be greatly enriched if you sell these excrements to the officials. Understand this!" Then the man, with respectful salutations, went away, carrying with him the two puppies, and came to his own house. Then he gave the puppies a little food at a time. When the gold puppy excreted, it excreted gold for him. When the silver puppy excreted, it excreted silver for him. The man greatly enriched himself by selling the metal.

Thereupon another man, for the sake of imitation, set his net in the river. He killed a quantity of fish. Then the raven came. The man smeared a fish with mud, and then threw it to the raven. The raven flew away with it. The man went after it, and at last, after going a long way, reached a large house. He went in there. The divine old man was very angry. He spoke thus: "You man are a man with a very bad heart. When you gave my daughter a fish, you gave it smeared all over with mud. I am very angry. Still, though I am angry, I will give you some puppies, as you have come to my house. If you treat them properly, you will be benefited." Thus spoke the divine old man, and gave a gold puppy and a silver puppy to the man. With a bow, the man went home with them.

The man thought thus: "If I feed the puppies

plentifully, they will excrete plenty of metal. It would be foolish to have them excreting only a little at a time. So I will do that, and become very rich." Thinking thus, he fed the puppies plentifully on anything, even on dirty things. Then they excreted no metal for him. They only excreted dirty dung. The man's house was full of nothing but dirty dung. As for the former man, who had received puppies from the divine old man, he fed his on nothing but good food, a little at a time. Gradually they excreted metal for him. He was greatly enriched.

Thus in ancient times, with regard to men who wished to grow rich, they could grow rich if their hearts were as good as possible. As for bad-hearted men, the gods became angry at all their various misdeeds. It was for this reason that, on account of their anger, even a gold puppy excreted nothing but dung. As for the house of that bad-hearted man, it grew so full of dung as to be too dirty for other people to enter. This being so, oh! men, do not be bad-hearted. That is the story which I have heard.

(Translated literally. Told by Ishanashte,
20th July, 1886.)

22. – *The Man who was changed into a Fox.*

A certain man's conduct was as follows: he went to every place, making it his business to do nothing but tell lies and extort things from people. Then, after a time, when wanting to extort again, he went on to another place. While walking along he used to think of what lies he could tell. Afterwards he heard a voice. It was not human language. He walked saying—"Pau! pau!"* When he looked at his own body, it was a fox's. Then he thought that, whether he might return to his own village, or go to another place, the dogs would kill him. So, with tears, he went away from the road into the mountains. There he found a large, leafy oak-tree.

He lay down crying beneath it. Then he fell asleep. He dreamt that there was a large house. He was outside of that house. A divine woman came out of it, and spoke thus: "Oh! what a bad man! what a villain! You have become a bad god, a devil, as a divine punishment for your misdeeds. Being thus made into a devil, why do you come and stand near my house? I should like to leave you alone. But as I am this tree, which is made the chief of trees by heaven, and as it would defile me to have you die beside my house, I will turn you into a man again and send you home. Do not misbehave yourself henceforth!" Thus spoke the divine woman.

Such was his dream. Meanwhile the branches at the top of the tree broke, and came crashing down, and he was greatly frightened. But when he started up, he was a man again. Then he worshipped the tree. Then he returned home. Then afterwards he did not misbehave. So also must you not misbehave, you men who live now!

(Translated literally. Told by Penri, 19th July, 1886.)

* An onomatopœia for the bark of the fox.

23. – The Rat Boy.

In a certain village there lived a very rich couple; but they were childless. They were very anxious for a child. But one day, as the wife went to the mountains to fetch wood, she found a little boy crying beside a tree. Rejoiced at this, she took him down with her to the village. Thenceforth they kept the boy with them. It was a place where there was plenty of deer and also of fish; it was a place provided with all the things which people like to eat. But though they hunted the deer, they could not catch them; though they angled for the fish, they could not catch them. They were very hungry. Hearing that great quantities both of fish and of deer were killed in the village next to theirs, towards the mountains, the wife went off to buy food there, taking the child with her. She went to the village next to theirs, towards the mountains. She went to the house of the chief.

The woman looked and saw fish hanging on poles, and flesh hanging on poles. With tears she longed for some. She went in, she went in to the chief's house. Then she stayed there. She was feasted on the best bits of the fish and on the best bits of the flesh. After that, as she lay down with her little boy, he rose quietly in the middle of the night. Then there was the sound of a rat nibbling at the fish and flesh on the poles. The woman thought it very strange. So at dawn the boy came quietly back, lay down by the woman's side, and slept there till the day was bright. The people of the house rose, and the chief went out and mumbled thus to himself: "Never were there such rats as this. There have been rats nibbling my good fish and my good flesh."

So the woman bought a quantity of fish and flesh and went off with it. She wanted the little boy to walk in front of her; but he disliked to do so. He would only walk after her. Then there was the sound of a rat nibbling at her load. When she looked back, the little boy was grinning. So they went on; they went home. Then she put both the fish and the flesh into the store-house. Then she whispered to her husband. Then her husband went into the next room, and made a trap. Then the trap was set in the store-house. Then they went to bed. The little boy lay between the woman and her husband; but after awhile he quietly rose and went out. He stayed away, without coming back. Daylight came. On the man of the house going into the store-house, there was a large rat in the trap. So he brought it down, beat it to death, and swept it on to the dust-heap. That night he had a dream. A person of divine aspect spoke to him thus; "You were childless, and wanting to have a child. The most wicked of the rats, seeing this, took the shape of a little boy, and dwelt in your house. For this reason, your village has been polluted. But as you have now killed the rat, all will now be right. I am sorry for you, so you shall have a child." Thus did he dream that the god spoke to him. As it was true, they got a child, though they had been childless.

For this reason, whether it be on the shore or in the mountains or anywhere else that one finds either a child or a puppy, one should not let it dwell in one's house without knowing its origin.

(Translated literally. *Told by Penri, 20th* July *1886.)*

24. – Don't throw Useful Things away.

A certain man had a little boy. A divine little boy and a divine little girl used to come and play with him every day. But the little boy alone could see them. His parents could not see them, but believed their child to be alone.

Now one day he fell ill, and during his illness his two playmates did not come to see him. Only at the very last did they come, when he seemed to be on the point of death. Then they came, and the little girl said: "We know the cause of your illness. Your grandfather possessed a beautiful axe. I myself am a small tray which he fashioned with that axe, and the little boy who comes with me is a pestle which was also fashioned with it. So the axe was our chieftain, and we are its children. But your father has been bad. He has thrown away the axe, which is now rusting under the floor. For this are you ill, in order to punish your father, because our chieftain the axe is angry. Therefore, as we were your playmates, we have come to warn you that, if you wish to live, you must tell your father to search for the axe, to polish it, to make a new handle for it, and to set up the divine symbols in its honour. Then may you be cured, and the axe too will pay you a visit in human shape."

So the boy told his father of this. The father thought that his son had been instructed in a dream. He searched under the floor of the house, and found the axe, and polished it, and made a new handle for it, and set up the divine symbols in its honour. Then his son was immediately healed.

After that, the axe (who appeared as a very handsome man), the tray, and the pestle all came, and became the little boy's brothers and sisters. The axe, being a god, knew all that went on and the causes of everything; and it and the tray and the pestle used always to tell the boy everything. Thus, if any one was sick, he knew why the sickness had come, and how it should be treated. He was looked upon as a great soothsayer and wizard, who could turn death into life. This was because other people only saw him. They did not see his divine informants, the axe, the tray, and the pestle.

For this reason never throw away anything that has belonged to your ancestors. You will be punished by the gods if you do so.

[In a variant of this tale, the death of child after child borne by a certain woman was owing to the fact that the doll with which she herself had played as a child (a piece of wood shaped like a bird) had been thrown away in the grass, and had thus had its anger aroused. A conversation on the subject between the spoon, the cup, and the iron chain whereby the kettle is hung over the fire from a hook in the ceiling, is overheard by a half-burnt piece of firewood, who warns the woman's husband in a dream. The doll is then looked for; and, when found, the divine symbols are set up in its honour. Thereupon the woman bears again. This time the child survives, to the delight of both its parents.]

(Written down from memory. Told by Ishanashte, 2nd December, 1886.)

25. – *The Wicked Wizard punished.*

One day a wizard told a man whom he knew that, if any one were to climb a certain mountain-peak and jump off on to the belt of clouds below, he would be able to ride about on them as on a horse, and see the whole world. Trusting in this, the man did as the wizard had told him, and in very truth was enabled to ride about on the clouds. He visited the whole world in this fashion, and brought back a map which he had drawn of the whole world both of men and of gods. On arriving back at the mountain-peak in Aino-land, he stepped off the cloud on to the mountain, and, descending to the valley, told the wizard how successful and delightful the journey had been, and thanked him for the opportunity kindly granted him of seeing sights so numerous and so strange.

The wizard was overcome with astonishment. For what he had told the other man was a lie, a wicked lie invented with the sole intention of causing his death; for he hated him. Nevertheless, seeing that what he had simply meant for an idle tale was apparently an actual fact, he decided to see the world himself in this easy fashion. So, ascending the mountain-peak, and seeing a belt of clouds a short way below, he jumped off on to it, but was instantly dashed to pieces in the valley below.

That night the god of the mountain appeared to the good man in a dream, and said: "The wizard has met with the death which his fraud and folly deserve. You I kept from hurt, because you are a good man. So when, obedient to the wizard's advice, you leapt off on to the cloud, I bore you up, and showed you the world in order to make you a wiser man. Let all men learn from this how wickedness leads to condign punishment!"

(Written down from memory. Told by Ishanashte, 21st July, 1886.)

26. – The Angry Crow.

A man came to a certain village—whence was not known,—dressed only in fine black robes. While he was there, some rice-beer was brewed. On being given some of it to drink, he was very joyful, and then danced. Then, as he went out-of-doors, he re-entered the house with a piece of hard dung in his mouth, and put it in the alcove. As the master of the house became angry and beat him, he, being a large crow, flew out of the window, making the sound "Kā! kā!" For this reason, even crows are creatures to be dreaded. Be very careful!

(Translated literally. Told by Penri, 11th July, 1886.)

[In another version of this story, communicated to me by Mr John Batchelor, the crow, enraged at not having received an invitation to a feast given by some of the more handsome birds, flies high into the air with a piece of hard dung in its mouth, and lets it drop into the middle of the party, to the great confusion of the guests. Some of the smaller birds take counsel together as to the advisability of interfering to restore the harmony of the occasion, but finally decide that it is not for them, who were also omitted from the list of invitations, to mix themselves up with such a matter. Moral: If you give a feast, ask all your friends to it. If any are left out, they are sure to feel hurt.]

27. – Okikurumi, Samayunguru, and the Shark.

Okikurumi and his henchman Samayunguru went out one day to sea, and speared a large shark, which ran away, up and down the sea, with the line and the boat. The two men grew very tired of pulling at him, and could not prevent the boat from being pulled about in all directions. Their hands were bloody and blistered both on the backs and on the palms, till at last Samayunguru sank dead in the bottom of the boat. At last Okikurumi could hold on no longer, and he cursed the shark, saying: "You bad shark! I will cut the rope. But the tip of the harpoons, made half of iron and half of bone, shall remain sticking in your flesh; and you shall feel in your body the reverberation of the iron and the scraping of the bone; and on your skin shall grow the rasupa-tree and the shiuri-tree of which the spear-handle is made, and the hai-grass by which the tip of the harpoon is tied to the body of it, and the nipesh-tree of which the rope tying the harpoon itself is made, so that, though you are such a mighty fish, you shall not be able to swim in the water; and you shall die, and a last be washed ashore at the river-mouth of Saru; and even the carrier-crows and the dogs and foxes will not eat you, but will only void their fœces upon you, and you shall at last rot away to earth."

The shark laughed, thinking this was merely a human being telling a falsehood. Okikurumi cut the rope, and, after a long time, managed to reach the land. Then he revived Samayunguru, who had been dead. And afterwards the shark died and was washed ashore at the river-mouth of Saru; and the tip of the harpoon made half of iron and half of bone had stuck in its flesh; and it had felt in its body the reverberation of the hammering of the iron and the scraping of the bone; and in its skin were growing therasupa-tree and the shiuri-tree of which the spear-handle used by Okikurumi was made, and the hai-grass by which the tip of the harpoon was tied to the body of it, and the nipesh-tree of which the rope tying the harpoon itself was made; and even the carrion-crows and the dogs and foxes would not eat the bad shark, but only voided their fœces upon him; and at last he rotted away to earth.

Therefore take warning, oh! sharks of the present day, lest you die as this shark died!

(Written down from memory. Told by Ishanashte, 24th November, 1886.)

III. – TALES OF THE PANAUMBE AND PENAUMBE CYCLE.*

28. – Panaumbe, Penaumbe, and the Weeping Foxes.

There were Panaumbe and Penaumbe. Panaumbe went down to the bank of a river, and called out: "Oh! you fellows on the cliff behind yonder cliff! Ferry me across!" They replied: "We must first scoop out a boat. Wait for us!" After a little while Panaumbe called out again. "We have no poles," said they; "we are going to make some poles. Wait for us!" After a little longer, he called out a third time. They replied thus: "We are coming for you, Wait for us!" Then the boat started, — a big boat all full of foxes.

So Panaumbe, having first seized hold of a good bludgeon, feigned dead. Then the foxes arrived, and spoke thus: "Panaumbe! You are to be pitied. Were you frozen to death, or were you starved to death?" With these words, all the foxes came up close to him, and wept. Thereupon Panaumbe brandished his bludgeon, struck all the foxes, and killed them. Only one fox did he let go, after breaking one of its legs. As for the rest, having killed them all, he carried them home to his house, and grew very rich [by selling their flesh and their skins].

---

* Panaumbe means "the person on the lower course of the stream." Penaumbe means "the person on the upper course of the stream." Conf. Aino "Memoir," p. 28.

Then Penaumbe came down to him, and spoke thus: "Whereas you and I were both equally poor, how did you kill such a number of foxes, and thereby become rich?" Panaumbe replied: "If you will come and dine with me, I will instruct you." But Penaumbe at once said: "I have heard all about it before." With these words he pissed against the door-sill, and went out.

Descending to the bank of the river, he called, crying out as Panaumbe had done. The reply was: "We are going to make a boat. Wait for us!" After a little while, he called out again. They replied: "We are going to make the poles. Wait for us!" After a little longer, they started,—a whole boatful of foxes. So Penaumbe first feigned dead. Then the foxes arrived, and said: "Penaumbe here is to be pitied. Did he die of cold? or did he die from want of food?" With these words, they all came close to Penaumbe and wept. But one fox among them, a fox who limped, spoke thus: "I remember something which once happened. Weep at a greater distance!" So all the foxes sat and wept ever further and further away. Penaumbe was unable to kill any of those foxes; and, as he brandished his bludgeon, they all ran away. He did not catch a single one, and he himself died a miserable death.

(Literal translation. Told by Ishanashte, 23rd July, 1886.)

29. – *Panaumbe, Penaumbe, the Fishes, and the Insects.*

There were Panaumbe and Penaumbe. Panaumbe went down to the sea-shore, squatted on the sand, pulled up his clothes, and, turning his back to the sea, opened his anus as widely as possible. Then all the whales and the salmon and the other good fishes, both great and small, thought it was a beautiful cavern in the rocks. They all swam towards it, and crowded into it. Panaumbe was much pleased. When his inside was quite full, he closed his anus and ran home. When he got to the house, he closed the door and the window. Then he opened his anus again, and let out all the whales and the salmon and the other good fishes, both great and small, so that the whole house was full of them. They could not swim away, because the door and window were shut. So Panaumbe caught them all. Some he ate, and some he sold. So he became a very rich man.

Then Penaumbe came down, and spoke thus: "You were poor before. Now you are very rich. How have you managed to get so rich?" Panaumbe said: "Come and dine with me. I can instruct you while we are eating." So, when Panaumbe had told Penaumbe how he had become rich, Penaumbe said: "I knew that before." With these words, he pissed against the threshold, and went out, – down to the sea-shore. Then he did as Panaumbe had told him, and opened his anus as wide as possible towards the sea. Then he felt all the whales and salmon and the other fishes, both great and small, crowding in. When his inside was quite full, he closed his anus, and ran home very quickly. When he got to the house he closed the door and the window, and stopped up even the smallest chinks. Then he opened his anus again, and let out all the whales and salmon, and the other good fishes, both great and small, so that the whole house was full of them. But when they came out, what had felt like whales and salmon, and all sorts of fishes, were really wasps and horse-flies and spiders and centipedes, and other poisonous insects, which stung him terribly. They could not get out, because Penaumbe had closed the window and the door, and had stopped up even the smallest chinks. So Penaumbe was stung to death by the wasps and centipedes and other poisonous insects which had come home in his inside. —

(Written down from memory. Told by Kannariki,
June, 1886.)

30. — Panaumbe, Penaumbe, and the Sea-Lion.

There were Panaumbe and Penaumbe. Panaumbe went down to the sea-shore, and walked up and down upon the sand. Then he saw a sea-lion in the water. He wanted to catch that sea-lion, and eat its flesh. So he called out to it: "Oh! Mr. Sea-Lion, if you will come here, I will pick the lice out of your head." The sea-lion was very glad to have the lice picked out of its head. So it swam to him. Then he pretended to pick the lice out of its head. But in reality he picked the flesh off its head, and the fat, and ate it. Then he said: "All the lice are picked off. You may go." After the sea-lion had swum a short way, it put its paw up to its head, in order to see whether the lice had really all been taken off. Then it felt that its flesh and fat were all gone, and that only the bones remained. So it was very angry, and swam back quickly towards the shore, to catch Panaumbe and kill him.

Panaumbe, when he saw the sea-lion pursuing him, ran inland towards the mountains. After running some time, he reached a place where the path divided. An old crow was perching on a tree there, and said: "Right or left! right or left! I see a clever man." The road to the right was broad, and the road to the left was narrow, because it was in a valley which ended in a point. Panaumbe thought thus: "If I take the broad path to the right, the sea-lion will overtake me, and kill me. But if I take the narrow path to the left, he will run so fast that he will get stuck at the end of the narrow valley, and I, being small, can slip out between his legs, and beat in his head from behind, and kill him." So Panaumbe ran along the narrow path to the left, and the sea-lion pursued him. But the sea-lion ran so heedlessly and quickly that it got stuck at the end of the narrow valley. Then Panaumbe slipped out between the sea-lion's legs, and beat in his head from behind, and killed him, and took home his flesh and his skin. Then Panaumbe became very rich.

Afterwards Penaumbe came down to him, and said: "You and I were both poor. How is it that you are now so rich?" Panaumbe said: "If you will come and dine with me, I will instruct you." So they went together to Panaumbe's house, where Panaumbe's mother, and his wife and children, were eating the flesh of the sea-lion. But Penaumbe, when he had heard what Panaumbe had done, said: "I knew that before." Then he stepped in the dishes set before Panaumbe's mother and wife and children, and spilt their food. Then he pissed on the threshold, and went away.

Penaumbe went down to the sea-shore, and saw a sea-lion, as Panaumbe had done. He called out to the sea-lion: "Oh! Mr. Sea-Lion, if you will come here, I will pick the lice out of your head." So the sea-lion swam to him. Then Penaumbe pretended to pick the lice out of its head. But in reality he picked the flesh and the fat off its head, and left nothing but the bones. The sea-lion felt a little pain, but thought that it was owing to the lice being picked out. So, when Penaumbe had finished picking and eating the flesh off its head, it swam away. But afterwards, feeling the pain more sharply, the sea-lion put its paw up to its head, and found that nothing but bone was left. So it was very angry, and swam back quickly towards the shore, to catch Penaumbe and kill him.

Penaumbe, when he saw the sea-lion pursuing him, ran inland towards the mountains. After running some time, he reached the place where the path divided. The old crow, which was perching on the tree, said: "Left or right! left or right! I see a fool." Penaumbe took the broad road to the right, in order to be able to run more easily. But the sea-lion ran more quickly than he could, and caught him and ate him up. Then Penaumbe died. But if he had listened to advice he might have become a rich man like Panaumbe.

(Written down from memory. Told by Kannariki, June, 1886.)

31. – *Panaumbe, Penaumbe, and the Lord of Matomai.**

Panaumbe wanted very much to become rich. For this reason, he stretched his penis across to the town of Matomai. Then the lord of Matomai spoke thus: "This is a pole sent by the gods; so it will be well to dry all the clothes upon it." So all the clothes and beautiful garments were dried. After a time Panaumbe drew back his penis, and all those clothes and beautiful garments came sticking to it. His house was greatly benefited. He became a very rich man.

Afterwards Penaumbe came down and said: "My dear Panaumbe, what have you done to become so rich?" Panaumbe said: "Come and eat, and I will tell you." Afterwards Penaumbe said: "This is the thing I intended to do. Abominable Panaumbe! bad Panaumbe! you have forestalled me." With these words, he pissed on the threshold, and went out. Then he went down to the sea-shore, and stretched his penis across the sea to Matomai. The lord of Matomai said: "This is a pole sent by the gods. It will be well to dry all the clothes and beautiful garments upon it." For this reason, all the clothes and beautiful garments were brought down, and put upon the divine pole. Penaumbe wanted to become rich quickly by drawing back his penis. So he drew it back quickly. The divine pole moved, and the lord of Matomai spoke thus: "It happened thus before. There was a pole sent by the gods. For this reason the clothes and beautiful garments were dried upon it. Then a thief stole the divine pole away. We all became poor. Now again our clothes and beautiful garments have been placed upon a pole. Now there seems to be

* The Aino pronunciation of Matsumae. Matsumae is a town in the south of Yezo. The lord or Daimyo resident there was formerly the chief Japanese authority in the country.

a thief again. Quickly cut the divine pole." For that reason the servants of the lord all drew their swords. They cut the divine pole, and all the clothes and beautiful garments were taken. Penaumbe was left with only half a penis. He drew it in. Then he had nothing. Then he became very poor. If Penaumbe had listened to Panaumbe's advice, he might have had food to eat, he might have become rich. But he did not like to listen to advice. For this reason he became poor.

(Translated literally.
Original communicated by Mr. John Batchelor, June, 1886;
also printed in "Aino Memoir," p. 133,
but with the indecent expressions softened down.)

32. – Drinking the Sea dry.

There was the Chief of the Mouth of the River and the Chief of the Upper Current of the River. The former was very vainglorious, and therefore wished to put the latter to shame, or to kill him by engaging him in the attempt to perform something impossible. So he sent for him, and said: "The sea may be a useful thing, in so far as it is the original home of the fish which come up the river. But it is very destructive in stormy weather, when it beats wildly upon the beach. Do you now drink it dry, so that there may be rivers and dry land only. If you cannot do so, then forfeit all your possessions." The other (greatly to the vainglorious man's surprise) said: "I accept the challenge."

So, on their going down together to the beach, the Chief of the Upper Current of the River took a cup, and scooped up a little of the sea-water with it, drank a few drops, and said: "In the sea-water itself there is no harm. It is some of the rivers flowing into it that are poisonous. Do you therefore first close the mouths of all the rivers both in Aino-land and in Japan, and prevent them from flowing into the sea, and then I will undertake to drink the sea dry." Hereupon the Chief of the Mouth of the River felt ashamed, acknowledged his error, and gave all his treasures to his rival.

(Written down from memory. Told by Ishanashte, 18th November, 1886.)

33. – *The Island of Women.*

In ancient days, an Aino chieftain of Iwanai went to sea in order to catch sea-lions, taking with him his two sons. They speared a sea-lion, which, however, swam off with the spear sticking in its body. Meanwhile a gale began to blow down from the mountains. The men cut the rope which was fast to the spear. Then their boat floated on. After some time, they reached a beautiful land. When they had reached it, a number of women in fine garments came down from the mountains to the shore. They came bearing a beautiful woman in a litter. Then all the women who had come to the shore returned to the mountains. Only the one in the litter came close to the boat, and spoke thus: "This land is woman-land. It is a land where no men live. It being now spring, and there being something peculiar to this country of mine you shall be taken care of in my house until the autumn; and in the winter you shall become our husbands. The following spring I will send you home. So now do you bear me to my house."

Thereupon the Aino chief and his sons bore the woman in the litter to the mountains. They saw that the country was all like moorland. Then the chieftainess entered the house. There was a room there with a golden netting, like a mosquito-net. The three men were placed inside it. The chieftainess fed them herself. In the day-time numbers of women came in. They sat beside the golden mosquito-net, looking at the men. At nightfall they went home. So gradually it got to be autumn. Then the chieftainess spoke as follows, "As the fall of the leaf has now come, and as there are two vice-chieftainesses besides me, I will send your two sons to them. You yourself shall be husband to me." Then two beautiful women came in, and led off the two sons by the hand, while the chieftainess kept the chief for herself.

So the men dwelt there. When spring came, the chieftain's wife spoke thus to him: "We women of this country differ from yours. At the same time as the grass begins to sprout, teeth sprout in our vaginas. So our husbands cannot stay with us. The east wind is our husband. When the east wind blows, we all turn our buttocks towards it, and thus conceive children. Sometimes we bear male children. But these male children are killed and done away with when they become fit to lie with women. For that reason, this is a land which has women only. It is called woman-land. So when, brought by some bad god, you came to this land of mine, there were teeth in my vagina because it was summer, for which reason I did not marry you. But I married you when the teeth fell out. Now, as the teeth are again sprouting in my vagina because spring has come, it is now impossible for us to sleep together. I will send you home to-morrow. So do you tell your sons to come here to-day in order to be ready."

The sons came. The chieftainess stayed in the house. Then, with tears streaming down her face, she spoke thus; "Though it is dangerous, to-night is our last night. Let us sleep together!" Then the man, being much frightened, took a beautiful scabbard in a bag in his bosom, and lay with the woman with this scabbard. The mark of the teeth remained on the scabbard. The next day dawned. Then the man went to his boat, taking his sons with him. The chieftainess wept and spoke thus: "As a fair wind is blowing away from my country, you, if you set sail and sail straight ahead, will be able to reach your home at Iwanai." So then the men entered their boat, and went out to sea. A fair wind was blowing down from the mountains, and they went along under sail. After a time they saw land; they saw the mountains about Iwanai. Going on for a time, they came to the shore of Iwanai. Their wives were wearing widows' caps. So their husbands embraced them. So the story of woman-land was listened to carefully. All the Ainos saw the beautiful scabbard which the chief had used with that woman.

(*Translated literally. Told by Penri, 17th July, 1886.*)

34. – *The Worship of the Salmon, the Divine Fish.*

A certain Aino went out in a boat to catch fish in the sea. While he was there, a great wind arose, so that he drifted about for six nights. Just as he was like to die, land came in sight. Being borne on to the beach by the waves, he quietly stepped ashore, where he found a pleasant rivulet. Having walked up the bank of this rivulet for some distance, he saw a populous place. Near the place were crowds of people, both men and women. Going on to it, and entering the house of the chief, he found an old man of very divine aspect. That old man said to him: "Stay with us a night, and we will send you home to your country to-morrow. Do you consent?"

So the Aino spent the night with the old chief. When next day came, the old chief spoke thus: "Some of my people, both men and women, are going to your country for purposes of trade. So, if you will be led by them, you will be able to go home. When they take you with them in the boat, you must lie down, and not look about you, but completely hide your head. If you do that, you may return. If you look, my people will be angry. Mind you do not look." Thus spoke the old chief.

Well, there was a whole fleet of boats, inside of which crowds of people, both men and women, took passage. There were as many as five score boats, which all started off together. The Aino lay down inside one of them and hid his head, while the others made the boats go to the music of a pretty song. He liked this much. After awhile, they reached the land. When they had done so, the Aino, peeping a little, saw that there was a river, and that they were drawing water with dippers from the mouth of the river, and sipping it. They said to each other: "How good this water is!" Half the fleet went up the river. But the boat in which the Aino was went on its voyage, and at last reached his native place, whereupon the sailors threw the Aino into the water. He thought he had been dreaming. Afterwards he came to himself. The boat and its sailors had disappeared—whither he could not tell. But he went to his house, and, falling asleep, dreamt a dream. He dreamt that the same old chief appeared to him and said: "I am no human being. I am the chief of the salmon, the divine fish. As you seemed in danger of dying in the waves, I drew you to me and saved your life. You thought you only stayed with me one night. But in truth that night was a whole year. When it was ended, I sent you back to your native place. So I shall be truly grateful if henceforth you will offer rice-beer to me, set up the divine symbols in my honour, and worship me with the words 'I make a libation to the chief of the salmon, the divine fish.' If you do not worship me, you will become a poor man. Remember this well!" Such were the words which the divine old man spoke to him in his dream.

*(Translated literally. Told by Ishanashte,
17th July, 1886.)*

35. – *The Hunter in Hades.*

A handsome and brave young man, who was skilful in the chase, one day pursued a large bear into the recesses of the mountains. On and on ran the bear, and still the young fellow pursued it up heights and crags more and more dangerous, but without ever being able to get near enough to shoot it with his poisoned arrows. At last, on a bleak mountain-summit, the bear disappeared down a hole in the ground. The young man followed it in, and found himself in an immense cavern, at the far end of which was a gleam of light. Towards this he groped his way, and, on emerging, found himself in another world. Everything there was as in the world of men, but more beautiful. There were trees, houses, villages, human beings. With these, however, the young hunter had no concern. What he wanted was his bear, which had totally disappeared. The best plan seemed to be to seek it in the remoter mountain district of this new world underground. So he followed up a valley;

and, being tired and hungry, picked the grapes and mulberries that were hanging to the trees, and ate them as he trudged along.

Happening suddenly, for some reason or other, to look down upon his own body, what was not his horror to find himself transformed into a serpent! His very cries and groans, on making the discovery, were turned into serpent's hisses. What was he to do? To go back like this to his native world, where snakes are hated, would be certain death. No plan presented itself to his mind. But, unconsciously, he wandered, or rather crept and glided, back to the entrance of the cavern that led home to the world of men; and there, at the foot of a pine-tree of extraordinary size and height, he fell asleep.

To him then, in a dream, appeared the goddess of the pine-tree, and said: "I am sorry to see you in this state. Why did you eat of the poisonous fruits of Hades? The only thing you can do to recover your proper shape is to climb to the top of this pine-tree, and fling yourself down. Then you may, perhaps, become a human being again."

On waking from this dream, the young man,—or rather snake, as he still found himself to be,—was filled half with hope and half with fear. But he resolved to follow the goddess' advice. So, gliding up the tall pine-tree, he reached its topmost branch, and, after hesitating a few moments, flung himself down. Crash he went. On coming to his senses, he found himself standing at the foot of the tree; and close by was the body of an immense serpent, ripped open so as to allow of his having crawled out of it. After offering up thanks to the pine-tree, and setting up the divine symbols in its honour, he hastened to retrace his steps through the long, tunnel-like cavern, through which he had originally entered Hades. After walking for a certain time, he emerged into the world of men, to find himself on the mountain-top, whither he had pursued the bear which he had never seen again.

On reaching his home, he went to bed, and dreamt a second time. It was the same goddess of the pine-tree, that appeared before him and said: "I have come to tell you that you cannot stay long in the world of men after once eating the grapes and mulberries of Hades. There is a goddess in Hades who wishes to marry you. She it was who, assuming the form of a bear, lured you into the cavern, and thence to the under-world. You must make up your mind to come away."

And so it fell out. The young man awoke; but a grave sickness overpowered him. A few days later he went a second time to Hades, and returned no more to the land of the living.

(Written down from memory. Told by Ishanashte, 22nd July, 1886.)

36. – *An Inquisitive Man's Experience of Hades.*

Three generations before my time there lived an Aino who wished to find out whether the stories told about the existence of an under-world were true. So one day he penetrated into an immense cavern (since washed away by the waves) at the river-mouth of Sarubutsu. All was dark in front, all was dark behind. But at last there was a glimmer of light a-head. The man went on, and soon emerged into Hades. There were trees, and villages, and rivers, and the sea, and large junks loading fish and seaweed. Some of the people were Ainos, some were Japanese, just as in the every-day world. Among the number were some whom he had known when they were alive. But, though he saw them, they,—strange to say,—did not seem to see him. Indeed he was invisible to all, excepting to the dogs; for dogs see everything, even spirits, and the dogs of Hades barked at him fiercely. Hereupon the people of the place, judging that some evil spirit had come among them, threw him dirty food, such as evil spirits eat, in order, as they thought, to appease him. Of course he was disgusted, and flung the filthy fish-bones and soiled rice away But every time that he did so the stuff immediately returned to the pocket in his bosom, so that he was greatly distressed.

At last, entering a fine-looking house near the beach, he found his father and mother,—not old, as they were when they died, but in the heyday of youth and strength. He called to his mother, but she ran away trembling. He clasped his father by the hand, and said: "Father! don't you know me? can't you see me? I am your son." But his father fell yelling to the ground. So he stood aloof again, and watched how his parents and the other people in the house set up the divine symbols, and prayed in order to make the evil spirit depart.

In his despair at being unrecognized he did depart, with the unclean offerings that had been made to him still sticking to his person, notwithstanding his endeavours to get rid of them. It was only when, after passing back through the cavern, he had emerged once more into the world of men, that they left him free from their pollution. He returned home, and never wished to visit Hades again. It is a foul place.

(Written down from memory. Told by Ishanashte,
22nd July, 1886.)

37. – *The Child of a God.*

There was a very beautiful woman, who was still without a husband. A man had already been fixed upon to become her husband, but he had not yet lain with her. Nevertheless the woman suddenly was with child. For this reason she was greatly surprised. As for other people, they thought thus: "She has probably become with child through lying with some other man." That was what other people said. The man who was to be her husband was very angry. But he could not know whence it was that she was with child.

Then she was delivered. She bore a little snake. She was greatly ashamed. Her mother took the little snake, went out, and spoke thus, with tears: "What god has deigned to beget a child in my daughter? Though he should deign to beget one, it would at least be well if he had begotten a human child. But this little snake we human beings cannot keep. As it is the child of the god who begot it, he may as well keep it." So saying, she threw it away. Then the old woman went in.

This being so, afterwards there was the noise of a baby crying. The old woman went out, and looked. It was a nice baby. Then the old woman carried it in. The woman who had given birth to the child rejoiced with tears. Then the baby was found to be a boy, and was kept. Gradually he grew big. After a time he became a man. Then, being a very fine man, he killed large numbers both of deer and of bears.

The woman who had given birth to him was alone astonished. What had happened was that, while she slept, the light of the sun had shone upon her through the opening in the roof. Thus had she become with child. Then she dreamt a dream, which said: "I, being a god, have given you a child, because I love you. When you die, you shall truly become my wife. Your and my son, when he gets a wife, shall have plenty of children." The woman dreamt thus, and worshipped. Then that son of hers, when pursued by the bears, could not be caught. He was a great hunter, a very rich man.

Then the woman died, without having had a human husband. Afterwards her son, getting a wife, had children, and became rich. His descendants are living to this day.

(Translated literally. Told by Penri,
21st July, 1886.)

38. – Buying a Dream.

A certain thickly populated village was governed by six chiefs, the oldest of whom lorded it over the other five. One day he made a feast, brewed some rice-beer, and invited the other five chiefs, and feasted them. When they were departing, he said: "To-morrow each of you must tell me the dream which he shall have dreamt over-night; and if it is a good dream I will buy it."

So next day four of the chiefs came and told their dreams. But they were all bad dreams, not worth buying. The fifth, however, did not come, though he was waited for at first, and then sent for several times. At last, when brought by force, he would not open his lips. So the senior chief flew into a rage, and caused a hole to be dug in front of the door of his own house, and had the man buried in it up to his chin, and left there all that day and night.

Now the truth was that the senior chief was a bad man, that the junior chief was a good man, and that this junior chief had forgotten his dream, but did not dare to say so. After dark, a kind god, — the God of the Privy, — came and said: "You are a good man. I am sorry for you, and will take you out of the hole." This he did; and, at that very moment, the chief remembered how he had dreamt of having been led up the bank of a stream through the woods to the house of a goddess who smiled beautifully, and whose room was carpeted with skins; how she had comforted him, fed him plenteously, and sent him home in gorgeous array, and with instructions for deceiving and killing his enemy, the senior chief. "I suppose you remember it all now," said the God of the Privy; "it was I who caused you to forget it, and thus saved you from having it bought by the wicked senior chief, because I am pleased with the way in which you keep the privy clean, not even letting grass grow near it. And now I will show you the reality of that of which before you saw only the dream-image."

So the man was led up the bank of a stream through the woods to the house of the goddess, who smiled beautifully, and whose room was carpeted with skins. She was the badger-goddess. She comforted him, fed him plenteously, and said: "You must deceive the senior chief, saying that the god of door-posts, pleased at your being buried near him, took you out, and gave you these beautiful clothes. He will then wish to have the same thing happen to him." So the man went back to the village, and appeared in all his splendid raiment before the senior chief, who had fancied him to be still in the hole,—a punishment which would be successful if it made him confess his dream, and also if it killed him.

Then the good junior chief told him the lies in which the badger-goddess had instructed him. Thereupon the senior chief caused himself to be buried in like fashion up to the neck, but soon died of the effects. Afterwards the badger-goddess came down to the village, and married the good man, who became the senior of all the chiefs.

(Written down from memory. Told by Ishanashte,
16th November, 1886.)

39. – *The Baby in the Box.*

There was once a woman who was tenderly loved by her husband. At last, after some years, she bore him a son. Then the father loved this son even more than he loved his wife. She therefore thought thus: "How pleasant it used to be formerly, when my husband loved me alone! But now, since I have borne him this nasty child, he loves it more than he does me. It will be well for me to make away with it."

Thus thinking, she waited till her husband had gone off bear-hunting in the mountains, and then put the baby into a box, which she took to the river and allowed to float away. Then she returned home. Later on, her husband came back; and she, with feigned tears, told him that the baby had disappeared — stolen or strayed, — and that she had vainly searched all round about the house and in the woods. The man lay down, like to die of grief, and refused all food. Only at length, when he saw that his wife, too, went without her food, did he begin to eat a little, fearing, in his affection for her, that she too might die of hunger. However, it was only when he was present that she fasted. She ate her fill behind his back.

At last, one day, not knowing what to do to rouse him, she said to him: "Look here! I will divert you with a story." Then she told him the whole story exactly as it had happened, being herself, all the while, under the delusion that she was telling him an ancient fairy-tale. Then he flew into a rage, took his bludgeon, beat her to death, and then threw her corpse out-of-doors. This was the way in which the gods chose to punish her.

Then the husband, knowing now that his search must be made down the stream, started off. At last, after seeking for a long time, he came to a lonely house, where he found a very venerable-looking old man, an old woman, and their middle-aged daughter, and also a boy. He said to the old man: "I come to ask whether you know anything of my little boy, who was placed in a box and set to float down the stream." The old man replied: "One day, when my daughter here went to draw water from the river, she found a box with a little boy in it. We knew not whether the child was a human creature, a god, or a devil. So doubtless he is yours. We have kept the box too. Here it is. You can judge by looking at it."

It turned out to be the same box, and the same boy. So the father rejoiced. Then the old man said: "Remain here. I will give to you for wife this daughter of mine, my only child. Live with us as long as my old wife and I remain alive. Feed us, and then you shall inherit from me." The man did so. When the old people died, he inherited all their possessions; and then, with his new wife and his beloved son, returned to his own village. So you see that, even among us Ainos, there are wicked women.

(Written down from memory. Told by Ishanashte, 17th November, 1886.)

40. – *The Bride Bewitched.*

There was once a very beautiful girl who had many suitors. But, as soon as she was married to one, and he lay down beside her and then stretched out his hand towards her vagina, a voice came from it, warning him to desist. This so much alarmed the bridegroom that he fled. This happened nine or ten times, till at last the girl was in despair; for none would now wed her, and her old father was put to shame. They plunged her into the water of the river, but it had no effect. So at last, in her grief, she ran to the mountains, and threw herself down at the foot of a magnolia-tree.

When, after some difficulty, she fell asleep, she dreamt that the tree was a house, outside of which she was lying, and from the window of which a lovely goddess popped out her head and said: "What has happened is in no way your fault. Your beauty has caused a wicked fox to fall in love with you. It is he who has got into your vagina, and who speaks out of it, in order to prevent the approach of any ordinary mortal husband. He, too, it is who has lured you out here, to carry you away altogether. But do not allow yourself to become subject to his influence. I will give you some beautiful clothes, and cause you to reach your house in safety. You must tell your father all about me." Then the girl awoke and went home. Her father exorcised the fox at last by carving an exact likeness of his daughter, and offering it to the fox with respectful worship. Then she married, and gave birth to children, and was happy all her life.

(Written down from memory. Told by Ishanashte, 17th November, 1886.)

41. – The Wicked Stepmother.

In ancient days, when men were allowed to have several wives, a certain man had two—one about his own age, the other quite young,—and he loved them both with equal tenderness. But when the younger of the two bore him a daughter, his love for his daughter made him also perhaps a little fonder of the mother of the child than of his other wife, to the latter's great rage. She revolved in her mind what to do, and at last feigned a grave illness, pretending not to be able even to eat, though she did eat when everybody's back was turned. At last, being to all appearance on the point of death, she declared that one thing alone could cure her. She must have the heart of her little step-child to eat.

On hearing this, the man felt very sad, and knew not what to do; for he loved this wicked wife of his and his little daughter equally dearly. But at last he decided that he might more easily get another daughter than another wife whom he would love as much as he did this one. So he commanded two of his servants to carry off the child to the forest while her mother was not looking, to slay her there, and bring back her heart. So they took her. But, being merciful men, they slew, instead of her, a dog that came by that way, and brought the child back secretly to her mother, who was much frightened to hear what had happened, and who fled with the child. Meanwhile the dog's heart was brought to the step-mother, who was so overjoyed at the sight of it, that she declared she required no more. So, without even eating it, she left off pretending to be sick.

For some time after this, she lived alone with her husband. But at last he was told of what had happened, and he grew very sullen. She, seeing this, wished for a livelier husband. So one day, when her husband was out hunting, a young man, beautifully dressed all in black, came and courted her, and she flirted with him, and showed him her breasts. Then they fled together, and came to a beautiful house with gold mats, where they slept together. But when she woke in the morning it was not a house at all, but a rubble of leaves and branches in the midst of the forest; and her new husband was nothing but a carrion-crow perching overhead, and her own body, too, was turned into a crow's, and she had to eat dung.

But the former husband was warned in a dream to take back his younger wife and his child, and the three lived happily together ever after. From that time forward most men have left off the bad habit of having more than one wife.

(Written down from memory. Told by Ishanashte, November, 1886.)

42. – *The Clever Deceiver.*

A long, long time ago there was a rascal, who went to the mountains to fetch wood. As he did not know how to amuse himself, he climbed to the top of a very thick pine-tree. Having munched some rice he stuck it about the branches of the tree, so as to make it look like birds' dung. Then he went back to the village, to the house of the chief, and spoke thus to him: "I have found a place where a beautiful peacock has its nest. Let us go there together! Being such a poor man, I feel myself unworthy of going too near the divine bird. You, being a rich man, should take the peacock. It will be a great treasure for you. Let us go!"

So the chief went there with him. When the chief looked, there truly were many traces of birds' dung near the top of the tall pine-tree. He thought the peacock was there. So he said: "I do not know how to climb trees. Though you are a poor man you do know how to do so. So go and get the peacock, and I will reward you well. Go and get the divine peacock!" So the poor man climbed the tree. When he was half way up it, he said: "Oh! sir, your house seems to be on fire." The chief was much frightened. Owing to his being frightened, he was about to run home. Then the rascal spoke thus: "By this time your house is quite burnt down. There is no use in your running there." The rich man thought he would go anywhere to die; so he went towards the mountains. After he had gone a short way, he thought thus: "You should go and see even the traces of your burnt house." So he went down there. When he looked, he found that his house was not burnt at all. He was very angry, and wanted to kill that rascal. Then the rascal came down. The chief commanded his servants, saying: "You fellows! this man is not only poor, but a very badly behaved deceiver. Put him into a mat, and roll him up in it without killing him. Then throw him into the river. Do this!" Thus spoke the chief.

The servants put the rascal into the mat, and tied it round tight. Then two of them carried him between them on a pole to the river-bank. They went to the river. The rascal spoke thus: "Though I am a very bad man, I have some very precious treasures. Do you go and fetch them. If you do so, it can be arranged about their being given to you. Afterwards you can throw me into the river." Hearing this, the two servants went off to the rascal's house.

Meanwhile a blind old man came along from somewhere or other. His foot struck against something wrapped up in a mat. Astonished at this, he tapped it with his stick. Then the rascal said: "Blind man! If you will do as I tell you, the gods will give you eyes, and you will be able to see. So do so. If you will untie me and do as I tell you, I will pray to the gods, and your eyes will be opened." The blind old man was very glad. He untied the mat, and let the rascal out. Then the rascal saw that, though the man was old and blind, he was dressed very much like a god. The rascal said: "Take off your clothes and become naked, whereupon your eyes will quickly be opened." This being so, the blind old man took off his clothes. Then the rascal put him naked into the mat, and tied it round tight. Then he went off with the clothes, and hid.

Shortly afterwards, the two men came, and said: "You rascal! you are truly a deceiver. So, though you possess no treasures, you possess plenty of deceit. So now we shall fling you into the water." The blind old man said: "I am a blind old man. I am not that rascal. Please do not kill me!" But he was forthwith flung into the river. Afterwards the two men went home to their master's house.

Afterwards the rascal put on the blind old man's beautiful clothes. Then he went to the chief's house and said: "My appearance of misbehaviour was not real. The goddess who lives in the river was very much in love with me. So she wanted to take and marry my spirit after I should have been killed by being thrown into the river. So my misdeeds are all her doing. Though I went to that goddess, I felt unworthy to become her husband, because I am a poor man. I have arranged so that you, who are the chief of the village, should go and have her, and I have come to tell you so. That being so, I am in these beautiful clothes because I come from the goddess." Thus he spoke. As the chief of the village saw that the rascal was dressed in nothing but the best clothes, and thought that he was speaking the truth, he said: "It will be well for me to be tied up in a mat, and flung into the river." Therefore this was done, just as had been done with the rascal, and he was drowned in the water.

After that, the rascal became the chief, and dwelt in the drowned chief's house. Thus very bad men lived in ancient times also. So it is said.

(Translated literally. Told by Ishanashte, *18th July, 1886.)*

43. – *Yoshitsune.*

[It has been generally believed, both by Japanese and Europeans who have written about the Ainos, that the latter worship Yoshitsune, a Japanese hero of the twelfth century, who is said, – not, indeed, by Japanese historians, but by Japanese tradition, – to have fled to Yezo when the star of his fortune had set. The following details concerning Yoshitsune bear so completely the stamp of the myth, that they may, perhaps, be allowed a place in this collection. It should be mentioned that Yoshitsune is known to the Ainos under the name of Hongai Sama. Sama is the Japanese for "Mr." or "Lord." Hongai is the form in which, according to a regular law of permutation affecting words adopted into Aino from Japanese, the word Hōgwan, which was Yoshitsune's official title, appears! The name of Hongai Sama is, however, used only in worship, not in the recounting of the myth. Mr. Batchelor, whose position as missionary to the Ainos must give his opinion great weight in such matters, thinks that the Ainos do not worship Yoshitsune. But I can only exactly record that which I was told myself.]

Okikurumi, accompanied by his younger sister Tureshi[hi], had taught the Ainos all arts, such as hunting with the bow and arrow, netting and spearing fish, and many more; and himself knew everything by means of two charms or treasures. One of these was a piece of writing, the other was an abacus; and they told him whence the wind would blow, how many birds there were in the forest, and all sorts of other things.

One day there came, – none knew whence, – a man of divine appearance, whose name was unknown to all. He took up his abode with Okikurumi, and assisted the latter in all his labour with wonderful ability. He taught Okikurumi how to row with two oars instead of simply poling with one pole, as had been usual before in Aino-land. Okikurumi was delighted to obtain such a clever follower, and gave him his sister Tureshi[hi] in marriage, and treated him like his own son. For this reason the stranger got to know all about Okikurumi's affair, even the place where he kept his two treasures. The result of this was that one day when Okikurumi was out hunting in the mountains the stranger stole these treasures and all that Okikurumi possessed, and then fled with his wife Tureshi in a boat, of which they each pulled an oar. Okikurumi returned from the mountains to his home by the seaside, and pursued them alone in a boat; but could not come up to them, because he was only one against two. Then Tureshi excreted some large fœces in the middle of the sea, which became a large mountain in the sea, at whose base Okikurumi arrived. But so high was it that Okikurumi could not climb over it. Moreover, even had not the height prevented him, the fact of its being nothing but filthy fœces would have done so. As for going round either side of it, that would have taken him too much out of the way. So he went home again, feeling quite spiritless and vanquished, because robbed of his treasures.

This is the reason why, ever since, we Ainos have not been able to read.

(Written down from memory. Told by Ishanashte,
25th November, 1886.)

V. – SCRAPS OF FOLK-LORE.

44. – The Good Old Times.

In ancient days, rivers were very conveniently arranged. The water flowed down one bank, and up the other, so that you could go either way without the least trouble. Those were the days of magic. People were then able to fly six or seven miles, and to light on the trees like birds, when they went out hunting. But now the world is decrepit, and all good things are gone. In those days people used the fire-drill. Also, if they planted anything in the morning, it grew up by mid-day. On the other hand, those who ate of this quickly-produced grain were transformed into horses.

(Written down from memory. Told by Ishanashte, November, 1886.)

45. – The Old Man of the Sea.

The Old Man of the Sea (Atui koro ekashi) is a monster able to swallow ships and whales. In shape it resembles a bag, and the suction of its mouth causes a frightfully rapid current. Once a boat was saved from this monster by one of the two sailors in it flinging his loin-cloth into the creature's open mouth. That was too nasty a morsel for even this monster to swallow; so it let go its hold of the boat.

(Written down from memory. Told by Ishanashte, July, 1886.)

46. – The Cuckoo.

The male cuckoo is called kakkok, the female tutut. Both are beautiful birds, and live in the sky. But in spring they come down to earth, to build their beautiful bottle-shaped white nests. Happy the man who gets one of these nests, and lets no one else see it. He will become rich and prosperous. Nevertheless, it is unlucky for a cuckoo to light on the window-sill and look into the house; for disease will come there. If it lights on the roof, the house will be burnt down.

(Written down from memory. Told by Penri, 16th July, 1886.)

47. – The [Horned] Owl.

There are six owls, — brethren. The eldest of them is only a little bigger than a sparrow. When perching on a tree, it balances itself backwards, for which reason it is called "The Faller Backwards." The youngest of the six has a very large body. It is a bird which brings great luck. If anyone walks beneath this bird, and there comes the sound of rain falling on him, it is a very lucky thing. Such a man will become very rich. For this reason the youngest of the six owls is called "Mr. Owl."

[The rain here mentioned is supposed to be a rain of gold from the owl's eyes.]

(Translated literally. Told by Penri, 16th July, 1886.)

48. – The Peacock in the Sky.

A cloudless sky has a peacock in it, whose servants are the eagles. The peacock lives in the sky, and only descends to earth to give birth to its young. When it has borne one, it flies back with it to the sky.

(Written down from memory. Told by Penri, July, 1886, and by Ishanashte, November, 1886.)

49. – Trees turned into Bears.

The rotten branches or roots of trees sometimes turn into bears. Such bears as these are termed payep kamui, i.e. "divine walking creatures," and are not to be killed by human hand. Formerly they were more numerous than they are now, but they are still sometimes to be seen.

(Written down from memory. Told by Penri, July, 1886.)

50. – Coition.

The Ainos think it very unlucky for the woman to move ever so slightly during the act of coition. If she does so, she brings disasters upon her husband, who is sure to become a poor man. For this reason, the woman remains absolutely quiet, and the man alone moves.

(Written down from memory. Told by Penri, July, 1886.)

51. – Birth and Naming.

Before birth, clothes are got ready for the expected baby, who is washed as soon as born.* The divine symbols are set up, and thanks are offered to the gods. Only women are present on the occasion. Generally in each village there are one or two old women who act as midwives.

The child may be named at any time. Ishanashte said that it was usually two or three months, Penri said that it was two or three years, after birth. The name chosen is usually founded on some circumstance connected with the child, but sometimes it is meaningless. The parent's name is never given, for that would be unlucky. How, indeed, could a child continue to be called by such a name when its father had become a dead man, and consequently one not to be mentioned without tears?

(Written down from memory. Told by Penri and Ishanashte, July, 1886.)

52. – The Pre-eminence of the Oak, Pine-tree, and Mugwort.

At the beginning of the world the ground was very hot. The ground was so hot that the creatures called men even got their feet burnt. For this reason, no tree or herb could grow. The only herb that grew at that time was the mugwort. Of trees, the only ones were the oak and the pine. For this reason, these two trees are the oldest among trees. Among herbs, it is the mugwort. This being so, these two trees are divine trees; they are trees which human beings worship.

Among herbs, the mugwort is considered to be truly the oldest.

Listen well to this, too, you younger folks!

(Translated literally. Told by Penri, 19th July, 1886.)

53. – *The Deer with the Golden Horn.*
(A specimen of Aino history.)

My very earliest ancestor kept a deer. He used to tie the divine symbols to its horns. Then the deer would go to the mountains, and bring down with it plenty of other deer. When they came outside the house my ancestor would kill the deer which his deer had brought from the mountains, and thus was greatly enriched. The name of the village in which that deer was kept was Setarukot.

There was a festival at a neighbouring village. So the man who kept the deer went off thither to the festival with all his followers. Only his wife was left behind with the deer. Then a man called Tun-uwo-ush [i.e. "as tall as two men"], from the village of Shipichara, being very bad-hearted, came in order to steal that deer. He found only the deer and the woman at home. He stole both the woman and the deer, and ran away with them. So the man who kept the deer, becoming angry, pursued after him to fight him. Being three brothers in all, they went off all three together. So Tun-uwo-ush invoked the aid of the whole neighbourhood. He called together a great number of men. Then those three brethren came together to fight him. As they were three of them, the eldest, having killed three score men, was at last killed himself. The second brother killed four score men, and was then killed himself. Then the youngest brother, seeing how things were, thought it would be useless to go on fighting alone. For this reason he ran away. Having run away, he got home. Having got home, he came to his house. Then he invoked the aid of all the neighbourhood. He invoked the aid even of those Ainos who dwelt in the land of the Japanese. Then he went off with plenty of men. Having gone off, he fought against Tun-uwo-ush. In the war, he killed Tun-uwo-ush and all his followers. Then he got back both the deer and the woman. That was the last of the Aino wars.

(Translated literally. Told by Ishanashte, 8th November, 1886.)

54. – *Dreams.*

To dream of rice-beer, a river, swimming, or anything connected with liquids, causes rainy weather. For instance, I dreamt last night that I was drinking rice-beer, and accordingly it is raining to-day.

To dream of eating meat brings disease. So does dreaming of eating sugar or anything red.

To dream of killing or knocking a man down is lucky. To dream of being killed or knocked down is unlucky.

To dream that a heavy load which one is carrying feels light is lucky. The contrary dream prognosticates disease.

To dream of a long rope which does not break, and in

which there are no knots even when it is wound up, is lucky, and prognosticates victory.

To dream of flying like a bird, and perching on a tree, prognosticates rain and bad weather.

When a man is about to start off hunting, it is very lucky for him to dream of meeting a god in the mountains, to whom he gives presents, and to whom he makes obeisance. After such a dream, he is certain to kill a bear.

To dream of being pursued with a sharp weapon is unlucky.

To dream that one is wounded, and bleeding freely, is a good omen for the chase.

To dream of the sun and moon is probably unlucky, especially if one dreams of the waning moon. But it is not unlucky to dream of the new moon.

To dream of a bridge breaking is unlucky. But to dream of crossing a bridge in safety is lucky.

For a husband to dream of his absent wife as smiling, well-dressed, or sleeping with himself, is unlucky.